GREATER
— IS —
COMING

How to Build Your Faith
through Fasting and Praying

DR. RUTH W. SMITH

GREATER
IS
COMING

How to Build Your Faith through Fasting and Praying

DR. RUTH W. SMITH

MEWE
Lithonia, GA

Publisher: MEWE, LLC
Lithonia, GA
www.mewellc.com

First Edition
ISBN: 979-8-9871970-0-4

For Worldwide Distribution
Printed in the USA

DEDICATION

To God the Father, God the Son, God the Holy Spirit, my beautiful children, including all my seed, the Body of Christ, Light of the World Christian Tabernacle International, Light of the World Covenant Fellowship International, and all of humanity that God so loved that He gave His Son to die for and His Spirit as a constant companion.

May we purpose to prepare for greater through FASTING AND PRAYING.

TABLE OF CONTENT

Introduction ix

What Happens When We Fast? 1

Faith Changes Everything 2

What Is Fasting? 5

Types of Fasting 8

    Normal Fasting 8

    Absolute Fasting 10

    Public Fasting 13

Conclusion 14

About the Author 17

Contact Information 19

INTRODUCTION

Most people try to push back the darkness through spiritual warfare; however, when it comes to fasting and praying as part of that warfare, there is a lukewarm response. But the truth is that fasting and prayer are key to your breakthrough. Add to that reading the Word and you have a powerful combination.

We see the value of fasting in Matthew 17 where Jesus' disciples were trying to cast a deaf and dumb spirit out of a boy, but they were unsuccessful. In previous encounters, they had seen the demons fleeing at their command; but this time it was different. After their failed attempts, Jesus, using His authority, rebuked the devil, and the child was delivered that very moment.

No wonder the disciples asked the Lord in private, *"Why could we not cast it out?"*

Note what Jesus said: *"This kind does not go out except by prayer and fasting"* (Matthew 17:21 NKJV).

There's an important principle underlying these words. Jesus wasn't talking about the demons leaving on account of prayer and fasting in and of itself. He was talking about demons recognizing the authority of someone who had faith. We know this because Jesus told the disciples they were ineffective because of their *"unbelief"* (verse 20). Then He went on to explain that this kind of demon can only be cast out through prayer and fasting – implying that prayer and fasting helps us build up our faith.

These are crucial times, and we all have to build up our faith. Nowhere in our history has the church been so vehemently attacked on all fronts worldwide as in our present time. But God Himself is our keeper, our champion. And if the Almighty God is with us, nothing in this world nor the powers of darkness can defeat us. We have to hold our ground no matter what. And if God has given us the keys to victory, then we have to arm ourselves with the weapons He tells us to use.

Throughout this booklet, we will examine some key points about fasting and praying to prepare for greater breakthroughs.

- Dr. Ruth W. Smith

WHAT HAPPENS WHEN WE FAST?

First, remember that fasting is a private, not a public matter. Jesus says in Matthew 6:16:

"Moreover when ye fast, be not, as the hypocrites, of a sad countenance: for they disfigure their faces, that they may appear unto men to fast. Verily, I say unto you, They have their reward" (KJV).

When we have to announce to the whole world that we are fasting, all we are ever going to get is the praises of men.

But here is what happens when you fast in secret:

"But thou, when thou fastest, anoint thine head, and wash thy face, That thou appear not unto men to fast, but unto thy Father which is in secret: and thy Father, which seeth in secret, shall reward thee openly" (verses 17-19).

In plain language, Jesus is saying, "Get up and look like you're going about your normal duties, so no one is aware that you are fasting. Only your heavenly Father knows in the secret place where you meet with Him. And your Father who sees you in secret will reward you openly."

I want to you to note here that just as Jesus finished talking about prayer and fasting, He went on to talk about how to handle our possessions. I believe that's relevant because this is a time when God wants to pour out His abundance on His people. But let us keep everything in balance. There is so much to thank God for in terms of material blessings, but if our well-being hinges on just having possessions, then our possessions will have us. Because they have us, we're never satisfied, and our craving for more can give way to lust. This involves, not just wrongful sexual desires, but the kind of lust that looks at everything, wants everything, and strives for everything. And so, as we fast, we discipline our flesh not to crave after things that our body demands but we learn to subjugate our flesh so that our spirit will lead us.

FAITH CHANGES EVERYTHING

So, let's go back to what Jesus said about fasting and faith. There are many things that we approach without faith. And because we do not have faith to believe for them, we make it seem as if God doesn't act on His promises. We claim that God said it, and then when it doesn't happen, we try to find an explanation. But here's the reality: we have to fast and pray to really hear the voice of God before we start making claims on promises.

When we have that confirmation in our spirit, we can declare a thing with confidence, and it's done. It's not in trying to manipulate the word or in manufacturing a miracle. It's not in making declarations enough times so we eventually believe them and convince other people too. Rather, it's something that God drops in your spirit. And once you have that confirmation, you can say with confidence, "God has said it – and it's settled."

Fasting and prayer therefore help us to center our minds on God's will so that we are not in our own desires, but we are in His desires.

Let me ask you a straightforward question now. Would you say that, in this phase of your life, you have embraced the entire process of following God's will? In other words, are you doing everything within your knowledge, power, and grace to follow through on what God is showing you? Can you say that in all honesty?

Many of us are already in transition and we're doing all we can to follow what God is saying. So, why do some of us feel like we're not progressing as fast as we should? Could it be due to a lack of understanding of what God is really saying?

Yes, many of us are going in a new direction and we can't go back. We are already in forward motion and we are not going to let anything stop us. The only thing that can block us is ourselves. It's our minds that cause us to doubt. So, if your mind tells you that you are not making progress, you need to align your thoughts with where God says you are. Make sure you're only doing what God instructs you to do. His plans for our life never fail.

When we speak of our own plan, we like to quote this scripture: ***"Delight yourself in the Lord and He will give you the desires of your heart"*** (Psalm 37:4 NIV). To many of us, that means if we delight ourselves in the Lord and if we desire a certain thing – a new car, a promotion, for instance – God is obliged to give it to us. No, that is a misrepresentation of the Word. What it really means is, "If I delight myself in the Lord, He will transform my heart to be more like His and have His desires." In other words, I will begin to desire what He wants for me. And, if He gives me the desire for something that's on His heart, He will provide the means to pursue it. That is very different from me chasing after my own dreams and trying to get God to come on board with me.

WHAT IS FASTING?

Essentially, fasting is self-denial by going without food for a period of time. Fasting may be total or partial. "Total" means avoiding food altogether, and "partial" means skipping certain meals or eating smaller portions at mealtimes. Since fasting is prescribed in both the Old and New Testament, we know that it has all along been a part of God's plan to empower His people. Fasting is so crucial to the children of God because when our faith is weak, fasting and prayer will strengthen our faith so we can stand up to the enemy's attacks – and this includes being tempted by our own passions and desires.

Fasting also tunes the mind to be sharp and alert. When you've had a full meal, you are probably not going to be ready for any kind of action. You just want to cruise in comfort and relax. Once you've eaten, your body goes into digestion mode, so you don't have as much mental energy to apply to other things. If you have a big day ahead of you, you don't really want to do a lot of eating. You should accomplish your project and then sit back and enjoy a full meal.

Well, that's also the way it is in the spirit when we are loaded with our worldly cares. We don't really have that leanness of spirit to stay alert and on our toes. So, the key is to stay sharp and remain in fasting and prayer. Therefore, fasting and prayer are critical to our spiritual development. In this transition phase, as you fast, you will grow at an accelerated rate. You will see things from a different perspective, and you will go deeper and dig new wells to establish a new reservoir of God in your soul. Transitioning is a state of movement from one stage to the next, but it is of no avail unless there is transformation of your mind as in Romans 12:2. What is wanted is a renewed mind, changed from the inside out.

Too many of us are constantly on the move physically but, in spite of all that activity, there's no change: we stay the same, our world stays the same. If your world stays the same, you will still find the same demons trying to block you, the same doubts, the same fork in the road where you haven't come to a decision. And fear and confusion still cloud your mind.

Many people admit they can't move because something is blocking them. In most cases the only thing that is trying to block you is yourself. You are your own enemy. Nothing else can stop you. Aren't you grateful that God gave His

Son for you? While you were nothing, while you were an enemy of God, He saw fit to give His Son for you because of His love. He also saw the potential in you and said, "I want to sow into you your future, even though right now you are standing as my enemy. I am seeing into your future, into what you can be if you give your life to Me. And I'm going to sow into your life, not because of your own merits but because of My Son."

Because God saw something beyond us, when we look at the ones we are led to share with, let us not see them as they are. Instead, see in them the hope of glory, see in them what they can be, where they can go, what God can do through them. See them through the blood of Jesus. However, if you say you are a follower of Christ and you do not have eyes to see their potential, you are missing the mark. If you don't look at potential, you will spend your whole life looking at people the way they are and wondering where they can go from here. Where's our hope if we can't see people in a better light than where they are today? Could we not see their future in Christ and say to them, "Right now, you don't have much but you'll have it all tomorrow. God already sees you in the future, and you look much better than you look right now."

We're living far below what we were made to be. We've set our sights on such small goals when there's a whole world out there that needs Jesus.

TYPES OF FASTING

Typically, when we think of fasting, we think of normal fasting where an individual abstains from food only, but there are different types of fasts that I will describe in this section.

Normal fasting

Normal fasting is abstaining only from food. In Luke 4:1-2 Jesus abstained from food in the wilderness for forty days. Here He was tempted by the devil, but the Bible also says that the Holy Spirit led him into this place of temptation. How many of you know that the Holy Spirit can lead you into temptation? Not because God needs to see what is in you – He already knows – but because He needs you to see the fight in you. You may have experienced many temptations, but when the Holy Spirit leads you into temptation, you don't fall into it. It's going to challenge your faith and entice you – but you know you're not giving in.

Jesus was tempted after fasting for forty days, but He responded to each temptation with one thing: the Word of God. When people bring their feelings and emotions into a situation, and not what the Word says, it can add to their confusion. Our feelings are not necessarily based upon truth. Of course, our feelings are important, and we need to be in tune with them, but they are not the final judge of the matter, and we ought to subject them to a higher standard.

You see, when you're just spewing out your feelings and emotions, you don't have any control over the situation. They're not going to help you get anything done and will lead you astray. No, when something comes up, find the appropriate Word just as Jesus did. See what the Word says about the situation first; then respond accordingly. When you find the appropriate Word, it will keep you in balance. You will rise above your human reactions. You will speak to your emotions until they are saturated with the truth, and you will have the victory.

So, we can fast as Jesus did for forty days if led by the Holy Spirit. During that time, it is the presence of God and the refueling and retooling you experience that will cause His glory to shine on your countenance. However long you decide to fast, what I want to charge you with is this: when a fast is called, commit yourself wholly to it. It's not so much for the church and assembly; it's for the individual.

Why are we fasting? We fast so that we can increase in our faith. We go walking out in faith, for the Bible says, *"everything that does not come from faith is sin"* (Romans 14:23). Regardless of how good a thing looks, or how good we look doing it, if it's not done in faith, it's sin. This verse should change your approach as you move forward in the things of God.

Absolute fasting

While normal fasting is abstaining from food, absolute fasting is abstaining from both food and water. That is not easy. Most people do not typically do an absolute fast because of dehydration. If you decide to go into this type of fast, let the Holy Ghost lead you into it. We do know that absolute fasting is necessary because in Acts 9:9, when Saul gave his life to Jesus on the road to Damascus, he was commanded to follow a three-day absolute fast. The radical change in him after that fast signaled a new name – from Saul to Paul.

While all change comes from the Word growing in you, fasting and prayer accelerates that growth. It makes you trust God and lean on Him. It makes you spend more time with Him. It makes you discipline your body to show who's in control. It helps us as the body of Christ to encourage and support one another.

I remember coming out of a fast being thankful that I had some people around me to help me eat right. If not for them, I could have given up a few times. My body was screaming for carbohydrates and fat – everything to indulge myself. The more I tried not to think about it, the more I wanted it. What seemed like such a simple thing became a battle with my flesh. The power to resist temptation was what God was trying to establish in my soul, and I would have missed it if I had allowed myself that distraction.

I know this kind of word will be punching at your fleshly self – only you don't even know you're getting punched because God is speaking directly to your spirit. He's speaking plainly. He's not addressing your mind. He's dealing with your soul and your spirit so that you can catch something that you can take away from this book. And when you finish, you won't be in the same place as when you started. What will change is you.

You see, when we deal with transitioning, it is not about moving from one place to another. Instead, it is a change from the inside. And when we change from the inside, we change our world. Your life should not be the same as it was yesterday.

Now the absolute fast is serious business. We have a record of how Moses went without food and water before he received the Ten Commandments on tablets of stone the second time (See Exodus 34:28). The first time he was so angered by his people that he broke them, and now he had to go back and receive a new set. I want to warn you, don't break your agreement with God. Don't break what you've already fasted for and possessed. Don't break what you've received from God!

If I could get that one thing in everybody's spirit, it is this: don't deviate from what you have already resolved. Don't make excuses that you gave in to people. You are not subject to all the people around you. You know what kind of people you should have around you – people that love God, enjoy the Holy Spirit, and speak life. These are the ones that steer you forward. In the long run, you may have to cut yourself off from some of your friends. By that I mean people who do not appreciate the things of the Spirit and hold you back. If you are still drawn to the same company, your fasting and praying will show you why you have to change! You have no strength within you. You're operating in your flesh. You're operating on the surface. God is working to build a person of substance that can stand some shaking. When the winds blow, they may bend; but you do not change direction.

So, fasting and prayer is a serious matter. It is not for those who are immature, unless they are ready to grow. This is not play time. There's a battle involved – but mainly the battle between your spirit and your flesh, but the outcomes are life changing.

Public fasting

Public fasting is where the entire congregation fasts for a specific reason and for a specific length of time. A public fast was called for in 2 Chronicles 20:1-3 because Israel was surrounded by enemy nations and was totally outnumbered.

It came to pass after this also, that the children of Moab, and the children of Ammon, and with them other beside the Ammonites, came against Jehoshaphat to battle. Then there came some that told Jehoshaphat, saying, There cometh a great multitude against thee from beyond the sea on this side Syria; and, behold, they be in Hazazontamar, which is Engedi. And Jehoshaphat feared, and set himself to seek the Lord, and proclaimed a fast throughout all Judah.

Rather than give in to fear and panic, King Jehoshaphat called for a collective fast and prayer to seek God's direction before they engaged with the enemy. God was so faithful that He sent His prophet to speak to Jehoshaphat to tell him the next step. The outcome was a reversal of the situation and victory for Israel.

Jehoshaphat's example tells us not to try to think through the problem with our minds, for this will only add fear and confusion. That's why we can't use the "Tell me how you feel" approach when we have to make critical decisions. No, get into the spirit to seek a God-inspired solution. Declare a fast for the whole assembly, and then check with one another about what the Lord has said. We don't hear the Lord when we're talking out of our emotions. No, we call a fast and prayer to seek God first, and then we talk about it.

CONCLUSION

Fasting is a spiritual exercise that involves self-sacrifice and subduing the demands of our body. The benefits are life changing. Fasting revives your spirit and brings you closer to God. Fasting is a time of consecration of your life and the issues in front of you. It requires us to surrender our own plan of action and spend this time with God asking Him for direction.

When we fast, we open ourselves to receiving God's desires for us that are much more fulfilling than our own – not our desires, not what would look good to people ... no, it should be all about Him. I promise you, when you decide on a plan of action with God's strategy, you will see your breakthrough unfold, and it will happen "without striving!" Yes, in Him we live and move and have our being ... so we should not be striving. If He says, "Take out your sword," then you take out the sword; it's a sweatless victory. But struggling and striving and pushing and prodding and prying and trying – it's just not the will of God. Rest in Him. Spend more time fasting and praying and a whole lot less fretting over what is or isn't. Only then will you see the true desires of your heart manifesting. So, prepare yourself for greater blessings through fasting and prayer. Hallelujah!

ABOUT THE AUTHOR

Dr. Ruth W. Smith, a native of Greensboro, Alabama, accepted Christ in 1964 and was filled with the Holy Spirit in 1981. She married Pastor Jimmie Lee Smith in 1982. Answering the call to the ministry in 1990, she co-founded Light of the World Christian Tabernacle International and Light of the World Covenant Fellowship International and was later ordained as a minister in 1991.

Under the dynamic leadership of Pastors Jimmie Lee and Ruth W. Smith, The Light grew from 400 to 1,500 members in a 4-year period until Archbishop Jimmie Lee Smith went home to be with the Lord in 2008. The stirring mission of the ministry is to "See a World Without Darkness."

Light of the World Covenant Fellowship International is an organization that mentors and empowers Pastors and Ministries throughout the world. Dr. Ruth was consecrated Archbishop of the organization on July 13, 2008 and became the first woman to serve a worldwide Diocese, overseeing ministries in 26 countries with a membership of over 200,000.

Dr. Ruth's passion for helping people advance the Kingdom of God started from an early age when she participated in the integration of schools in Hale County, Alabama. Through her leadership at The Light, she champions community support through food and clothing drives. In 2013, she received the "Torch Bearer" award by the Southern Christian Leadership Conference (SCLC) in Washington, DC, in recognition of her many years of work as a scholar and spiritual leader committed to the legacy of SCLC founder, Dr. Martin Luther King, Jr.

She recently opened the Jimmie Lee Smith Community Center (JLSCC), which provides Sports, Education and Entertainment to the surrounding communities. Additionally, she established three SateLight locations: LOTW Decatur, December 2015; LOTW South, April 2016; and LOTW Gwinnett, December 2016.

Dr. Ruth holds a Master's degree in Biblical Counseling and a Doctorate in Ministry from Biblical Life College and Seminary in Marshfield, Missouri. She is the published author of five other books, *A Word on Love*, *Keep Moving*, *Rules of Encouragement, The Voice,* and *Generosity Is the Heart of God*.

She is the proud mother of five children, twelve grandchildren and four great-grandchildren, whom she dearly loves. She is anointed to preach and teach the gospel of Jesus Christ, which she does readily worldwide. Her foundational scripture is Romans 8:28, *"For we know that all things work together for good to them that love God, to them who are the called according to His purpose."*

CONTACT INFORMATION

Ministry
Light of the World Christian Ministries
5883 Highway 155 North
Stockbridge, GA 30281
678.565.7001
thelight@comeintothelight.org
www.comeintothelight.org

Purchasing
678.565.7001
www.comeintothelight.org

Publisher
MEWE, LLC
404.482.3135
mewecorporation@gmail.com
www.mewellc.com